Texas
Wildflowers

A beginner's
field guide to
the state's most
common flowers

Interpreting the Great Outdoors

Text by Beverly Magley, Illustrations by DD Dowden

FALCON®

GUILFORD, CONNECTICUT
HELENA, MONTANA
AN IMPRINT OF THE GLOBE PEQUOT PRESS

A FALCON GUIDE ®

ISBN 1-56044-386-3

On the front cover: Texas bluebonnet (the state flower), Texas prickly pear, meadow beauty, and fire wheel.

Botanical Consultant: Jackie Poole

Library of Congress Cataloging-in-Publication Data is available.

Printed in Korea
First Edition/ Seventh Printing

CAUTION
The Globe Pequot Press assumes no liability for accidents happening to or injuries sustained by readers who engage in the activities described in this book.

Contents

Introduction

Zing! The brilliant yellow and deep red colors of a wildflower grab your attention. On bent knee to look more closely, you can sniff the lovely fragrance and admire the beauty. While there, it's easy to notice more flowers, tiny and shy, tucked close to the earth. Shiny green leaves have many shapes and sizes, and the world of flowering plants becomes more interesting. Some plants are just poking up through the ground. Others have tightly furled buds not yet ready to open. Still others are in full bloom.

Flowering plants have existed for about 120 million years. They started evolving when dinosaurs roamed the earth. Flowers are unique because each of their seeds has a protective, nourishing shell that helps the seed survive.

The sweet nectar of wildflowers entices nectar-drinkers that pollinate the blossoms. The pollinated blossoms then produce seeds. A nice trade! So when you see a bee or an ant crawling inside a flower or watch a hummingbird or butterfly sip nectar, remember they are essential to the survival of flowers. In addition to providing food, flowers may provide shelter for insects and other little creatures.

Texas has more than 5,000 species of flowering plants. Different wildflowers have learned to live in the special conditions created by such varied habitats as the salty Gulf Coast, shady thick forests, or dry open plains. Texas is so big and has so many different kinds of habitats that we have divided the state into nine distinct regions, to help you locate the wildflowers more easily.

Flowers have common names, like our nicknames, that often tell something about them. Devil's claw, spider lily, and Indian paintbrush are descriptive names. But these names can be confusing because many flowers have several common names. To eliminate confusion, learn the scientific names. The scientific name is usually descriptive, too, but uses Latin words instead of English. Once you know some of the main features of a flower family, it gets easier to name individual members of that family.

Lie on your back and look at a flower as it splashes color up to the sky. Turn onto your side and get an ant's-eye view of the world. Then go belly-down to see how many different plants are growing right under your nose. It's amazing!

Habitat Regions of Texas

1. High Plains
2. Rolling Plains
3. Blackland Prairies
4. Oak Woodlands and Cross Timbers
5. Pineywoods
6. Gulf Coast and Marshes
7. South Texas Plains
8. Edwards Plateau
9. Trans-Pecos

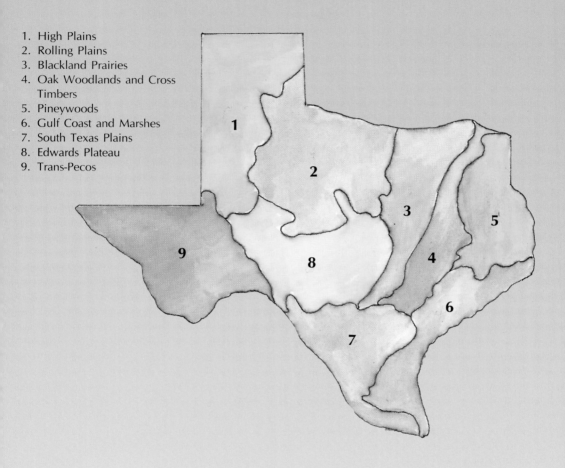

Varied terrain divides Texas into different habitats for plants and animals.

Pineywoods

Pretty streams tumble through the hills in eastern Texas. The woods are mostly evergreen pine trees, but there are also some hardwoods that lose their leaves each winter. Look for wildflowers in the sunny clearings, in the swamps, and out on the grassy, open forest floor. You might see a shy wild turkey peeking out from a thicket or hear woodpeckers tapping on a tree. Try a game of pine-cone baseball. All you need is a stick for a bat and fallen cones for the balls.

Meadow Beauty

other names: none
height: 4 to 24 inches
season: May to September

The long, yellow, curved anther sticks out of the pinkish or white petals. This edible plant is quite delicious. The sour leaves taste good in salads, and the tubers taste sort of like nuts.

Rhexia mariana

Slender Trillium

other names: Wake Robin, Birthroot
height: 4 to 12 inches
season: March to May

"Tri" in the name trillium means three, just as it does in the word triangle. This plant has three large green leaves, three white petals that turn pinkish with age, three sepals, three styles, and three reddish berries. Trillium has the common name wake robin because it blooms early in the spring—about when the first robins arrive. Ants love the trillium's oil-rich seeds and help scatter them throughout the forest. If you pick the bloom from a trillium, the plant may die or not bloom again for years.

Birdfoot Violet

other names: Violet
height: 4 to 6 inches
season: March to April

There are more than 300 species of violets in the world, and they come in many colors. The lower, larger flower petal forms a landing platform for bees. Violets are edible. The leaves have lots of vitamins A and C, and the blossoms are sometimes used to make candy, jelly, and syrup. The leaves look a little like the print left by a bird's foot.

Viola pedata

Trillium gracile

Prairie Iris

other names: Purple Pleatleaf
height: 1 to 2 feet
season: April to October

The leaves have folds that look like long, narrow pleats. The blossom has purplish petals and tiny brown dots on the yellow center. Each flower grows from a corm that has dark brown scales.

Eustylis purpurea

May Apple

other names: Mandrake
height: 12 to 16 inches
season: March to April

The flower looks like an apple blossom blooming between two big umbrella-like leaves. The roots, leaves, and seeds are poisonous, but you can make the bitter gold fruits into a flavorful jelly. Raccoons like to eat the fruit, too.

Cardinal Flower

other names: Scarlet Lobelia
height: 1 to 3 feet
season: May to December

These blossoms are scarlet-red like the bright plumage on a cardinal. The color attracts hummingbirds and sulphur butterflies, which come and feed on the nectar.

Podophyllum peltatum

Lobelia cardinalis

Pitcher Plant

other names: Yellow Trumpets
height: 1 to 2 feet
season: March to April

Sweet nectar on the edge of the pitcher-shaped leaf entices insects. A bug can easily crawl down the tube, but tiny, barbed, downward-pointing hairs on the inside of the leaf prevent it from climbing back out. When the insect falls into the bottom of the "pitcher," plant fluids and bacteria digest the unlucky critter.

Jack-in-the-Pulpit

other names: Indian Turnip
height: 1 to 3 feet
season: March to June

Some people think this plant looks like a preacher standing in a fancy, old-fashioned covered pulpit. The striped spathe forms a little roof to protect the flowering spadix. Gently lift the spathe: The plant is female if the flowers look like tiny green berries. If the flowers have little threadlike stamens and are dropping pollen, the plant is male. Insects fly from plant to plant and spread the pollen. Indians cooked and ate the corm of this plant.

Cancer Weed

other names: Lyreleaf Sage
height: 8 to 36 inches
season: December to May

The square stem says that this is a member of the mint family. The leaves are used for medicinal purposes, such as brewing a tea to aid digestion or gargling with the tea for a sore throat. Lyreleaf refers to the shape of the leaves, which look somewhat like old-fashioned lyres, or harps.

Salvia lyrata

Arisaema triphyllum

Sarracenia alata

Purple Coneflower

other names: Coneflower
height: 4 to 20 inches
season: May to September

This drooping flower is best appreciated through a magnifying glass. The long slender cone is covered with tiny brown tubular disk flowers—more than you can count. A few scraggly purple ray flowers stick out of the bottom of the cone. People know many medicinal uses for this plant. Indians made tea from the flowers and leaves or boiled the flower heads to make a rust-colored clothing dye.

False Dragonhead

other names: Obedient Plant
height: 3 to 7 feet
season: June to August

Do these flowers look like dragons' heads to you? Some people think they do. Gently move the flower stalk and see if it "obediently" stays where you put it.

Texas Thistle

other names: none
height: 1 to 6 feet
season: March to September

Pale lavender flowers adorn a stem bearing numerous spiny leaves. Thistle seeds ride the wind on feathery little parachutes and often inhabit areas where the ground has been disturbed. A legend tells why a thistle is the national emblem of Scotland. One night long ago, the Danes invaded Scotland and took off their boots to sneak up on a village. One soldier stepped on a thistle and yelled in pain, and the villagers awoke in time to defend themselves and their country.

Echinacea purpurea

Physostegia digitalis

Cirsium texanum

9

Oak Woodlands and Cross Timbers

Post oak and blackjack oak trees rise above the tall grasses on the pretty hills of eastern Texas. The best time to find wildflowers blooming is after a rainstorm, usually in May and June.

There are lots of birds and animals to see in the woodlands. Overhead, turkey vultures soar on the warm air rising from the hot ground. Busy squirrels scamper around, playing and storing acorns for the winter. Other wildlife, such as deer and turkeys, eat the acorns, too. The mockingbird is the Texas state bird. Its scientific name means "many tongues," and you'll know why after you hear it imitate other birds. Scissor-tailed flycatchers swoop down off powerlines to catch insects in midair.

Maypop

other names: Passionflower
height: vine climbs to 25 feet
season: April to August

This blossom often pops open in May. Its other common name refers to Easter, which is sometimes called "The Passion of Christ." Early Spanish explorers thought the flower head and fringed edges represented Christ on the cross with a crown of thorns. After blossoming, the edible, lemon-colored, egg-shaped fruit has an odd, sweet flavor.

Wine Cup

other names: Poppy Mallow
height: 8 to 39 inches
season: February to June

The cup-shaped blossom is the color of burgundy wine. A Greek story tells of a servant trying to cheer his ruler by dancing with a cup of wine. The servant danced so long and hard he fell down and dropped the cup. This plant grew where the wine spilled.

Blazing Star

other names: Gayfeather
height: 8 inches to 5 feet
season: August to October

Blazing stars look like lavender exclamation points in a meadow. Flowers cluster on each stiff, hairy stem and bloom from the tip of the stem down. Feathery purplish styles stick gaily out of each flower, and little glands dot the leaves. Indians ate the tubers, which can grow sixteen feet into the ground. Some people think the tuber can cure the effects of a rattlesnake bite. Others disagree.

Callirhoe involucrata

Liatris elegans

Passiflora incarnata

Fire Wheel

other names: Indian Blanket
height: 8 to 20 inches
season: March to September

Each flower is like a fiery pin-wheel. It can blanket a field in showy colors. Look closely at the blossom, called a composite: the brightly colored pinwheel parts are called ray flowers, and the center disk is composed of dozens of tightly packed in-dividual florets. One legend tells of a great Indian weaver who was buried with his most beautiful blanket. The Great Spirit was pleased with the blanket and caused flowers of the same colors to grow and spread across the land.

Wild Indigo

other names: none
height: 12 to 18 inches
season: March to April

The large yellow blossoms are so heavy they nod toward the earth. When the leaves dry out, they turn a dark indigo blue. Some people tie a few sprigs of wild indigo to their horse's tail to repel flies. Wild indigo has many medicinal properties and has been used to treat typhus, scarlet fever, and other illnesses.

Texas Stork's Bill

other names: Wild Geranium,
Texas Filaree
height: 4 to 24 inches
season: February to April

Look for the delicate pink- or purple-tinged veins in the white or pink petals. The long-beaked seedpods that appear after the flower fades and falls resemble a stork's bill. Each style is attached to a seed. The styles twist like a corkscrew to help the seeds separate and disperse. If a fruit pod is ripe and still closed, touch it gently and watch the tiny cups fling seeds through the air.

Gaillardia pulchella

Baptisia leucophaea

Erodium texanum

11

Sundew

other names: none
height: 4 to 12 inches
season: February to August

Each sundew leaf looks like a round green sun with little shiny rays. When insects investigate this plant, the leaf hairs fold over and the bug gets stuck in the gooey drops. The sundew takes several days to suck the nutritious juices from an insect. Then the leaf opens up, and the bug skeleton dries up and blows away. Yuck!

Ironweed

other names: Flat Top
height: 2 to 5 feet
season: June to September

Butterflies love to sip the nectar of these purple disk flowers. You might also see other long-tongued insects feasting on this sweet member of the thistle family. The plant forms so many branches it appears to have a flat top above the tough stem.

Meadow Pink

other names: Texas Star, Prairie Rose Gentian, Marsh Pink
height: 3 to 20 inches
season: April to July

These showy flowers really grab your attention. Star-shaped, deep pink blossoms decorate moist meadows and streambanks. Look in the center of the bloom to find the tiny yellow star.

Drosera annua

Vernonia baldwinii

Sabatia campestris

Standing Cypress

other names: Texas Plume,
    Red Texas Star
eight: 2 to 5 feet
season: May to September

Scarlet, trumpet-shaped flowers flare into little stars. A whole colony of these showy, tall plumes standing in a field is a beautiful sight. Some people think the little leaves look like the leaves of a cypress tree. Hummingbirds find this a tasty treat.

Spiderwort

other names: Spider Lily
height: 4 to 31 inches
season: March to September

The arching leaves look like the splayed legs of a spider. Spiderwort's delicate flowers bloom in the morning, and by afternoon they have turned into a jellylike blob. This plant is especially sensitive to radiation and may help warn us about dangerous pollution.

Horse Mint

other names: Spotted Beebalm,
    Wild Bergamot
height: 1 to 3 feet
season: May to July

Gently feel the stem of this plant. Mints have square stems. The leaves can be used to make tea. Texas beekeepers believe mint is the most important plant for their honey business. Wild animals and cattle like horse mint, but horses don't. Maybe we should change the name to deer mint!

*Monarda
punctata*

*Ipomopsis
rubra*

Tradescantia spp.

13

Blackland Prairies

Prairie wildflowers must survive high winds, hot sun, and long periods with no rain. Many have evolved a very short life cycle and can grow, blossom, and produce seeds in just a few weeks. Some prairie plants have a waxy or hairy surface, which helps them preserve precious moisture. Others only open their blossoms in the cooler evenings or early mornings.

Large herds of bison used to graze the prairie. Today, almost all of the prairie has either been plowed into cropland or is grazed by livestock. Look for prairie wildflowers in cemeteries, along railroad tracks and country roads, and in unused fields.

While scouting for prairie wildflowers, listen to the song of a meadowlark, look for the flickering colors of butterflies, and watch the red-tailed hawks fly low as they search for rodents.

Maximilian's Sunflower

other names: none
height: 1 to 8 feet
season: September to November

Prince Maximilian of Weid (now Germany) explored the United States in the early 1800s. He identified many plants no one had ever seen before, including this species of sunflower. The scientific name *Helianthus* means "a sun plant" because the big blossoms turn to face the sun all day. Birds and rodents love to eat wild sunflower seeds.

Snow-on-the-Prairie

other names: none
height: 8 to 39 inches
season: July to October

White margins on the upper leaves look like a dusting of snow on each plant. The tiny flower is not showy. Don't pick any of this plant, because the milky sap may irritate your skin. Other members of this family include poinsettias and rubber trees.

Euphorbia bicolor

Bluebell Gentian

other names: none
height: 1 to 2 feet
season: June to September

These remarkable, blue, bell-shaped blossoms close at night or when it rains. Perhaps the gentian dislikes water in its cup. Indians and settlers used the roots of the gentian to make a tea to treat indigestion and other ailments. The blossoms open in the morning and close for the cool nights. *Eu* and *stoma* are from the Greek words for "good mouth." Perhaps the Greeks thought the blossom was opening its mouth to sing!

Eustoma grandiflorum

Helianthus maximiliani

Blue Larkspur

other names: Espulela del
      Caballero (Cowboy's Spur)
height: 20 to 40 inches
season: April to July

   The spur at the base of each
blossom is like the long hind
claw on a lark's foot: larkspur.
Its scientific name comes from
a Greek tale that tells of a
fisherman who died saving a
dolphin. In gratitude, King
Neptune transformed the man's
body into a flower bud shaped
liked a dolphin and colored the
blue of the sea. The word
delphinium means dolphin.

Compass Plant

other names: White Rosinweed
height: 1 to 3 feet
season: June to September

   Pretty daisylike flowers perch
atop round, stout stems.
Perhaps this is called a com-
pass plant because the blossom
faces the sun all day, moving
from east to west.

Wild Petunia

other names: none
height: 4 to 32 inches
season: April to October

   Trumpet-shaped, purplish
blossoms open to greet the
sunrise, then wilt in the
evening. These flowers look a
lot like the garden petunias
around town. When the
seedpods dry and split, they
throw the seeds several yards
away. Listen! You might hear
them popping some quiet
evening.

Delphinium
carolinianum

Silphium
albiflorum

Ruellia
humilis

Gulf Coast and Marshes

Rivers and creeks wind slowly through this mostly level countryside on their way to the Gulf of Mexico, creating bogs, swamps, and marshes. The Atlantic Ocean sends rain and fog over the coast, where moisture-loving trees, shrubs, and flowers grow in abundance. Some flowers hug the ground on sandy beaches, while others take refuge in thickets. Many have roots that extend deep into the ground, both for stability and to find water in sandy soil.

You can look for seashells, build sand castles, and watch fiddler crabs scuttle sideways across the sand. Red-winged blackbirds sing from the marshes, alligators hide in freshwater marshes, and whooping cranes, gulls, and seabirds fish for their meals.

Spider Lily

other names: none
height: 20 to 32 inches
season: March to May

Six narrow petals droop around the inner cup like the long rounded legs of a spider. Real spiders have eight legs, though. The bulb may be dormant for years until conditions are just right. Then this lovely lily sends up its beautiful blossom. The scientific name *Hymenocallis* means beautiful membrane, referring to the plant's delicate cuplike flower.

Hymenocallis liriosme

Shore Purslane

other names: none
height: sprawling vine
season: all year

Purslane grows on the salty ocean shore. Its dark reddish-purple blossoms rise above the juicy leaves. People like to eat the young shoots. You can boil the coastal purslane to get some of the saltiness out.

Saltmarsh Morning Glory

other names: none
height: 2 to 5 inches
season: June to November

The rolled-up flower buds unfurl into lovely, funnel-shaped blossoms that smell very sweet while blooming. They twist again as they wilt. These flowers grow on sand dunes and beaches. The thick, leathery leaves help the plant preserve moisture in its dry, sandy environment.

Ipomoea sagittata

Sesuvium portulacastrum

Blue-Eyed Grass

other names: none
height: 2 to 20 inches
season: most of the year

The leaves look like grass, but this plant is actually in the iris family. The flower stalk is twisted, and each blossom lasts only a day. But the plant puts out one after another and attracts bees over a long growing season. The scientific name *Sisyrinchium* comes from a Greek word meaning "pig snout," because pigs love to root in the ground and eat the bulb.

Sisyrinchium spp.

Beach Evening Primrose

other names: Drummond
　　　　　Sundrops
height: 1 to 3 feet
season: March to November

The fragile yellow blossoms unfold in the evening, awaiting pollination by night-flying insects. If you see one open in the morning, perhaps it's still waiting for an insect. Some nocturnal moths sleep in the closed blossoms during the day. Look for wings sticking out of the flower. Primroses produce as many as 6,000 seeds, and goldfinches love to gobble them.

*Oenothera
drummondii*

Cattail

other names: Bulrush
height: 4 to 10 feet
season: April to May

Ever had a cattail pancake? Indians used every part of this plant. The pollen makes a flour for pancakes, breads, or cakes; the leaves can be woven into baskets; the downy seeds are good insulation and make good pillow stuffing or absorbent padding for diapers; and the roots are edible.

*Typha
domingenis*

South Texas Plains

Mesquite, granjeno, and cactus are associated with the dry southern plains. Despite harsh and variable conditions, the desert hosts delicate wildflowers and succulent cacti, spiny shrubs and hardy trees. Jackrabbits, javelinas, crested caracaras, bobwhite quail, ocelots, rattlesnakes, coyotes, and horned lizards are all shy, secretive residents of the desert.

Many of the wildflowers are annuals, growing each year from a seed into a beautiful flower in just a few weeks. Rather than try to endure the blistering heat or freezing cold of the seasons, they let their tough seeds await a gentle rain. Sometimes they have to wait several years before conditions are right. Then they quickly germinate, grow, blossom, and produce more seeds.

Texas Lantana

other names: Calico Bush,
    Herba de Cristo
height: 1 to 4 feet
season: March to November

Yellowish-orange and orangish-red blossoms cluster on the tips of this shrub. Some of the stems are horribly prickly, and perhaps that is why *horrida* is part of its name. This adaptable plant can grow in swamps, in chaparral, in the woods, and along dry roadsides.

Lantana horrida

Rain Lily

other names: none
height: 6 to 12 inches
season: May to September

This fragrant bloom pops open a few days after a heavy rain. The flaring blossom begins to open in the evening, and by noon the next day it has opened completely. After the plant has flowered, the paper-thin seeds scatter on the wind.

Cooperia pedunculata

Red Prickly Poppy

other names: Spiny Prickle-Poppy
height: 1 to 3 feet
season: February to April

It's a good thing these leaves are so prickly that livestock won't touch them: the whole plant is quite poisonous. The pinkish or blood-red flower petals blow off in the wind, leaving just the bunch of yellow stamens on the branch.

Argemone sanguinea

Turk's Cap

other names: Red Mallow
height: 1 to 5 feet
season: most of the year

This blossom reminds some people of a Turkish fez, or cap. The stamens stick out of the twisted red petals. The edible fruit of this plant looks like a tiny red apple. Hummingbirds like the nectar, and the fruit is a favorite of songbirds.

Malvaviscus drummondii

Texas Prickly Pear

other names: Tuna Cactus
height: 8 inches to 7 feet
season: February to June

Prickly pear is an abundant and widely distributed cactus throughout Texas. Its tasty fruit, called a "tuna," is a burgundy-colored, juicy, pear-shaped treat enjoyed by both humans and animals. Be sure to peel off the miniscule spines, called glochids, before eating the fruit.

Opuntia lindheimeri

Yucca

other names: Spanish Dagger, Soapweed
height: leaves 1 to 3 feet, blossom 5 to 20 feet
season: March to June

Clusters of bell-shaped flowers dangle from the tall stalks. The yucca is a very useful plant. The buds, flowers, and fruit can be eaten; the roots and stems make a good washing soap; and the tough, fibrous leaves can be pounded, dried, and woven into rope, sandals, mats, and baskets.

Yucca treculeana

19

Edwards Plateau

This high, hilly plateau supports junipers, oaks, and mesquite trees. Deer browse on the shrubs and grasses, sharing the forage with cattle, sheep, and goats. The streams and rivers have carved many canyons through this plateau. Cypress trees and pretty ferns grow along the wet streambanks in the canyons. Catfish, turtles, and people like to swim in the clear, cool streams.

Climb one of the live oaks and sit very still. Perhaps you'll hear an armadillo rustling the dead leaves, looking for something to eat. Or maybe a canyon wren will serenade you with its beautiful song. Painted buntings have plumage more colorful than many wildflowers.

Snapdragon Vine

other names: none
height: twining vine to 7 feet
season: February to October

Snapdragon vines crawl along the ground or climb dry rock walls. Gently squeeze the sides of a blossom to watch it snap open like a dragon ready to roar.

Angel Trumpets

other names: none
height: 1 to 3 feet
season: March to October

White trumpet-shaped flowers open in the late afternoon or evening to attract night-flying insects. Hawk moths have long tongues that can reach down the long tube to reach the sweet nectar.

Texas Bluebonnet

other names: Lupine, Wolf Flower, El Conejo (the Rabbit)
height: 4 to 16 inches
season: March to May

Bluebonnets are the state flower of Texas. Their seeds are harvested commercially and sold for garden use. *Lupus* is Latin for "wolf," so named because early people thought lupine gobbled up nutrients in the soil. But today we know that wolves are a positive part of the natural world, and we've also learned that *Lupinus* actually enriches the soil it inhabits.

Maurandya antirrhiniflora

Acleisanthes longiflora

Lupinus texenis

20

Indian Paintbrush

other names: Paintbrush
height: 10 to 30 inches
season: March to October

Look carefully for the narrow pale-green flowers hidden among the bright red, orange, or yellow bracts. The roots of a paintbrush can burrow into the roots of a different plant, such as sagebrush, and then steal part of its food. Because of that ability, paintbrush is called a root parasite.

Castilleja spp.

Mexican Hat

other names: Prairie Coneflower
height: 1 to 2 feet
season: May to October

Some people think the blossom resembles a tall, broad-brimmed Mexican hat. This flower is best appreciated through a magnifying glass. The long slender cone is covered with tiny, brown, tubular disk flowers—more than you can count. A few scraggly yellow or purple ray flowers stick out the bottom of the cone. Indians made tea from the flowers and leaves or boiled the flower heads to make a rust-colored clothing dye.

Ratibida columnifera

Phlox

other names: Wild Sweet William
height: 2 to 6 inches
season: March to May

The sweet scent of phlox is especially fragrant at sunset. The blossom's narrow tube invites butterflies and other long-tongued flying insects to the nectar, but the sticky stem discourages crawling insects such as ants. In 1835, T. Drummond sent phlox seeds from Texas back to a gardening society in England, and the plant flourished. Today we plant hybrids of that Texas phlox in our own gardens.

Phlox drummondii

21

Trans-Pecos

The Trans-Pecos region has many different types of habitat. There are dry desert sand dunes, high wooded mountains, and low grassy valleys. This region has many flowers that grow nowhere else in Texas.

Watch as hummingbirds search for red, tubular, nectar-rich flowers. Cactus wrens build tiny nests in the shelter of the spiny cactus. Roadrunners, pack rats, mountain lions, and mule deer also inhabit this region. Try a hike to the cool, tree-covered mountaintops for a view of the vast desert floor.

Claret Cup Cactus

other names: Hedgehog Cactus
height: 2 to 20 inches
season: April to July

Gorgeous scarlet flowers sometimes cover the entire plant. Each blossom may stay open for three to five days. Claret cup cacti usually grow in clumps, hugging close to their neighbors. They have so many spines they look as bristly as a hedgehog.

Cholla

other names: Cane Cactus
height: 3 to 10 feet
season: April to August

Beautiful magenta flowers bloom on this oddly shaped cactus. Its tubular stems grow every which way, giving it very interesting outlines. Indians cooked and ate the spineless fruits. Deer and cattle munch on them, too. A dried cholla stem has lots of holes along it and is often used for handicrafts.

Candelilla

other names: Wax-Plant
height: 1 to 2 feet
season: May to October

Little white flowers with reddish centers cluster at the ends of the stems. Boiling and refining the plant produces a very good wax with many uses, such as making soap, candles, ointments, shoe polish, and varnish. Mexican people know of medicinal uses, and the fibrous stem can be used to make a high-quality paper. What a useful plant!

Euphorbia antisyphilitica

Opuntia imbricata

Echinocereus triglochidiatus

Agave

other names: Lechuguilla,
Century Plant
height: leaves 1 to 3 feet,
flower stalks 6 to 15 feet
season: May to August

Agave plants store up their food for twelve or more years, then produce a huge flower stalk that can grow as much as eighteen inches each day. When the blossoming is over, the plant is all used up and dies. The needle-sharp leaf tips really hurt if you walk too close to this plant. Deer and javelina like to eat the tender offshoots and young flower stalks of the agave.

*Agave
lechuguilla*

Ocotillo

other names: Devil's Walking Stick
height: 3 to 20 feet
season: March to August

Scarlet blossoms adorn the tips of these skeletal shrubs each spring. Ocotillo has nasty thorns that make a good barrier fence. If there are leaves on the stems, you'll know there is moisture in the ground. Otherwise the plant drops its leaves to wait out the dry spells. Apache Indians dried and ground the roots to use as a medicine to reduce swelling.

*Fouquieria
splendens*

Prairie Flax, Chihuahua Flax

other names: Blue Flax
height: 4 to 24 inches
season: April to September

Fragile petals often blow away in the afternoon breeze, but new blossoms will open the next morning. Flax stems are very useful fibers. The Egyptians wrapped their mummies in cloth of flax. Indians made ropes and fishing lines. We make linen thread and cloth from a cultivated flax. And flaxseed oil, also known as linseed oil, is an important part of some paints, varnishes, linoleums, and inks.

*Linum lewisii
Linum vernale*

High Plains

This high, flat plateau was once covered with grasslands. Now it's mostly cropland. After a good rain, many "playa lakes" fill with water. Migrating birds such as ducks and geese like the playas. You'll find lots of flowers around the playas that can't grow out in the drier plains nearby. Watch for antelope springing along as they run for cover. They look like they're on pogo sticks!

Common Sunflower

other names: Annual Sunflower
height: 8 inches to 8 feet
season: March to October

One sturdy plant can have as many as thirty flower heads reaching toward the sunshine. Sunflowers are very useful plants. You can make a pretty yellow dye from the flowers or a darker blue-black dye from the seeds. Birds and rodents love the tasty sunflower seeds. Indians made thread from the fibrous stems.

Aster

other names: Tahoka Daisy
height: 4 to 20 inches
season: June to October

Aster is the Greek word for "star." We've formed many words from it: astronomy, astrology, asterisk, asteroid, and astronaut, to name a few. Most of the 600 species of asters are native to North America. According to one myth, asters were created from star dust. What a nice thought! Aster blossoms are composed of the inner yellow disk flowers and the purplish outer ray flowers. They are pretty planted in gardens.

Scarlet Globemallow

other names: none
height: 4 to 16 inches
season: May to October

Globemallow belongs to the mallow family, which has more than a thousand species. Marshmallows were once flavored with the juice of one kind of mallow. Okra is the edible part of another mallow species. Cotton is yet another kind of mallow. What a lot of diversity in one family!

Sphaeralcea coccinea

Machaeranthera tanacetifolia

Helianthus annuus

olling Plains

Below the Texas Panhandle, little creeks and streams cut through the hilly, rolling plains. The bright sandstone cliffs provide a pretty contrast to the dark green junipers and pale green mesquites.

Kangaroo rats use their tails to balance when they bound along the ground like a real kangaroo. Great blue herons are common near streams and stock ponds. A killdeer may drag her wing as though it's broken, to trick you into following her away from her streamside nest.

Pink Sensitive Brier

other names: Shame Vine
height: runners of 2 to 4 feet
season: April to June

The leaflets are so light-sensitive they fold up at night and if the weather gets cloudy. They even close if you touch them. The blossom looks like a pink ball atop a prickly stem. Some people think they look like magical fairy dusters. Can you make up a story about these little, pink, puff-ball blossoms?

Schrankia uncinata

Butterflyweed

other names: Orange Milkweed, Chiggerflower
height: 8 to 39 inches
season: April to September

Butterflies love the nectar in these clustered, bright orange blossoms. Long ago, people chewed the roots to treat lung problems and used the fluffy seeds to stuff pillows. Some people decorated their hats with the feathery seeds. Some cooks put the tender young pods in their stew.

Asclepias tuberosa

Yarrow

other names: Milfoil, Thousand Seal
height: 1 to 3 feet
season: June to September

Yarrow is very aromatic and has many medicinal uses. The scientific name *Achillea* was chosen because the famous Greek hero Achilles used yarrow to treat his wounded soldiers. Properly prepared, yarrow can help stop bleeding, increase perspiration and break a fever, and ease a rash.

Achillea millefolium

Roadside and Disturbed Areas

People have a way of disrupting natural plant communities. We bulldoze roads, dig ditches, build railroads, and make trails. We build homes and plant garden flowers that go to seed and sprout somewhere else.

Sometimes fires, manmade or natural, burn an area, or a flooding river rushes through. All these disturbances create unique conditions that many plants find too harsh. But some plants, often thought of as weeds, are able to grow and flourish. Many of these plants are an important part of nature because they stabilize the soil with their roots, add needed nutrients, and prepare the way for grasses, shrubs, and trees to grow in the disturbed area again someday.

Next time you see a tall mullein or prickly thistle growing beside the road, remember its essential role of healing the area.

Queen Anne's Lace

other names: Wild Carrot, Bird's Nest
height: 1 to 3 feet
season: April to July

In the 1700s, Queen Anne of England wore this pretty plant instead of cloth lace. The central pinkish flower might be a drop of her blood when she pricked her finger sewing the plant to her collar. This is an ancestor of today's garden carrot.

Daucus carota

Buffalo Gourd

other names: Stinking Gourd, Coyote Melon, Chili Coyote, Calabazilla
height: up to 1 foot, with stems u to 20 feet long
season: May to August

Yellow blossoms often hide under the hairy, triangular leaves, but the awful-tasting fruits, or gourds, are easy to see in winter when the leaves have died. Coyotes eat the gourds, and people dry and paint them for house ornaments. Early settlers crushed the roots of the plant to make soap.

Cucurbita foetidissima

Jimsonweed

other names: Thorn Apple
height: 1 to 5 feet
season: May to October

Sit by a jimsonweed some evening and watch the flower buds slowly unfurl into trumpet-shaped blossoms. The puff of fragrance from each bloom must be the sweetest aroma in the world. Jimsonweed has big, coarse, gray-green leaves that don't smell very nice, as well as a prickly round fruit. Don't eat any part of this plant! Even though it's related to the potato, it's quite poisonous.

Datura spp.

Goldenrod

other names: none
height: 1 to 5 feet
season: August to October

Some people once believed that if you carried this plant around, you would find treasure in the earth. And so they named it goldenrod. A goldenrod plant has 10 to 20 dark gold flower heads. Butterflies love its sweet nectar. Indians used it in steam baths to help ease pain, and its Latin name also reflects its medicinal qualities: *Solidago* means "to heal." Goldenrod gets blamed for hay fever, but that is usually caused by a similar-looking plant called ragweed.

Woolly Mullein

other names: Cow's Lungwort
height: 4 to 39 inches
season: March to November

Yellow blossoms cluster around the top of mullein's tall spike, and starburst-shaped hairs grow so densely the whole plant appears woolly. Hummingbirds use the soft hairs to line their tiny nests. Ancient Romans and Greeks dipped the tall stalks in tallow to make torches. This plant was once used to treat cows with lung problems.

Unicorn Plant

other names: Devil's Claw,
    Ram's Horn
height: 1 to 2 feet
season: May to September

This plant has hitchhiking seeds! The fruit has a clawlike hook that catches a ride on passing deer or livestock. When the fleshy fruit disintegrates and spills out the seeds, the leftover woody shell has a long, curved horn, like a unicorn's horn. Some people pickle and eat the young fruit pods.

Solidago spp.

Proboscidea louisianica

Verbascum thapsus

27

Conclusion

"Over here! Look at me!" shout the bright colors of a wildflower. The showy blossoms attract us, but more importantly they attract insects and other flying and crawling visitors that pollinate each flower. Bees, moths, beetles, butterflies, hummingbirds, even ants and bats are essential for the wildflowers to make seeds.

When you bend down to enjoy the sweet smell of a fresh blossom, remember to share the space with other creatures. Wildflowers may like us to look at them, but they depend on their other visitors for survival.

Glossary

Alternate	Not opposite each other
Annual	A plant that lives for one season
Anther	The part of the stamen containing pollen
Basal	Near the base, at the bottom
Berry	Fleshy fruit containing seeds
Biennial	A plant that lives for two years, blooming only the second year
Bract	Leaflike scale
Bulb	A plant storage organ, usually below the ground
Corm	Bulblike underground swelling of a stem
Composite	Flower head composed of a cluster of ray and disk flowers
Disk flower	Tubular floret in the center part of a composite flower head
Evergreen	Bearing green leaves throughout the year
Filament	The stalk of the stamen
Floret	A small flower that is part of a cluster
Flower	Part of a plant containing male and/or female reproductive parts
Flower head	A dense cluster of flowers atop a stem
Fruit	Seed-bearing part of a plant; ripened ovary
Habitat	The place where a plant naturally grows and lives
Head	A dense cluster of flowers atop a stem
Herb	A plant with no woody stem above ground
Irregular	Not symmetrical in shape
Nectar	Sweet liquid produced by flowers to attract insects
Opposite	A pair of leaves opposite each other on a stem
Ovary	Part of the pistil that contains the developing seeds
Parasitic	Growing on and deriving nourishment from another plant

Pathfinders	Lines on a plant that guide insects to the nectar
Pedicel	Supporting stem of a single flower
Perennial	A plant that lives from year to year
Petals	Floral leaves inside the sepals that attract pollinators
Petiole	The stem supporting a leaf
Pistil	Seed-bearing organ of a flower
Pollen	Powderlike cells produced by stamens
Ray flowers	The flowers around the edge of a flower head; each flower may resemble a single petal
Regular	Alike in size and shape
Rhizome	Underground stem or rootstock
Saprophyte	A plant that lives on dead organic matter
Seed	Developed female egg
Seedpod	Sac enclosing the developed female egg(s)
Sepal	Outermost floral leaf that protects the delicate petals
Shrub	Low woody plant, usually having several stems
Spadix	Fleshy spike that bears flowers
Spathe	Leafy covering connected to the base of a spadix
Spur	Hollow appendage of a petal or sepal
Stamen	Pollen-producing organ of a flower
Stigma	The end of the pistil that collects pollen
Style	The slender stalk of a pistil
Succulent	Pulpy, soft, and juicy
Tendril	Slender, twining extension of a leaf or stem
Tuber	Thickened underground stem having numerous buds
Whorl	Three or more leaves or branches growing from a common point

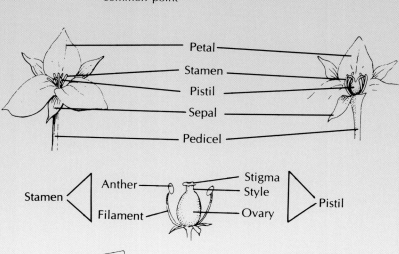

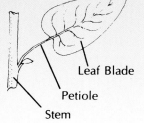

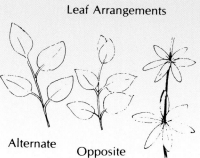

Leaf Arrangements

Leaf Blade

Petiole

Stem

Alternate

Opposite

Whorl

Where to See Wildflowers in Texas

Wildflowers can be found anywhere in Texas, but some of the best places are state and federal parks, forests, refuges, and recreation areas. Many of these areas have campgrounds, picnic areas, nature trails, and interpretive services to help visitors see and appreciate these lands and their wildflowers.

These state parks are especially good places to view wildflowers:

Seminole Canyon
Caddo Lake
Lake Corpus Christi
Copper Breaks
Caprock Canyon
Palo Duro Canyon
Monahans Sandhills
Hueco Tanks
Palmetto

State natural areas:

Lost Maples
Enchanted Rock
Lake Brownwood
Big Bend Ranch

The Nature Conservancy preserves:

Clymer Meadow Preserve
Sandylands Preserve

City wildflower locations:

National Wildflower Research Center, Austin
Mercer Arboretum and Botanic Gardens, Houston
Zilker Park, Austin
San Antonio Botanical Center, San Antonio

National parks, forests, and refuges:

Big Bend National Park
Guadalupe Mountains National Park
Padre Island National Seashore
Santa Ana National Wildlife Refuge
Aransas National Wildlife Refuge
Laguna Atascosa National Wildlife Refuge
Matador Wildlife Management Area
Amistad National Recreation Area
Big Thicket National Preserve
Davy Crockett National Forest
Angelina National Forest
Sabine National Forest
Sam Houston National Forest